STEAM PORTFOLIOS 8

WEST SOMERSET RAILWAY

Richard Jones

First published 1992

ISBN 0 7110 2110 4

Published by Ian Allan Ltd, Shepperton, Surrey; and
printed by Ian Allan Printing Ltd at their works at
Coombelands in Runnymede, England.

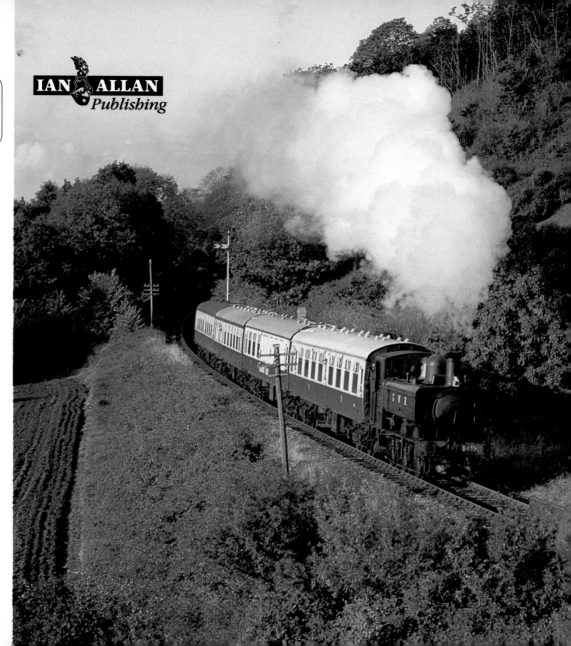

Front cover: By Great Western to the sea side...
GWR '61xx' '2–6–2T' No 6106 passes Blue
Anchor Bay with the 3.45pm Bishops Lydeard
to Minehead on June 1991. *Brian Dean*

Back cover: The West Somerset Railway at its
very best... GWR '64xx' '0–6–0PT' No 6412
awaits departure from Blue Anchor with the
12.03pm Williton to Minehead goods on 5
September 1990. *Bryan Hicks*

Pannier at Castle Hill

Right: Castle Hill, between Williton and
Stogumber, is one of the most popular
photographic locations on the West Somerset
Railway. In beautiful autumn sunlight GWR
'64xx' '0–6–0PT' No 6412 passes with a
Bishops Lydeard bound train. A beautifully
recreated Great Western branch line scene.
Peter Doel

Introduction

The West Somerset Railway Company was authorised by Act of Parliament in 1857, to build a railway from a junction with the B&ER at Norton Fitzwarren, two miles west of Tauton, to the town and harbour at Watchet, a distance of 14½ miles. Built to the designs of Isambard Kingdom Brunel and laid out to his broad gauge, the railway was opened in March 1862.

Several years later the Minehead Railway Company drew up plans to build a line from an end on junction at Watchet through to Minehead. Again built to broad gauge, the line was opened in July 1874, thus giving the line as we know it today.

Both sections of the line were worked first by the Bristol & Exeter Railway, and later by the Great Western Railway, and both were converted to standard narrow gauge over one weekend in October 1882. Traffic for the first 30 years or so was not particularly heavy, but increased with the development of Minehead as a holiday and seaside resort. A number of improvements were made to the branch during the 1930s. British Railways took over responsibility for the line in January 1948. With increased motor car ownership the line began to decline and was closed in January 1971.

Efforts to preserve and reopen the Taunton to Minehead branch commenced even before the line had actually closed. In May 1971 a new West Somerset Railway Company was incorporated, actively supported by the West Somerset Railway Association. In August 1973 Somerset County Council bought the whole line from Norton Fitzwarren to Minehead and leased it back to the railway company. Train services commenced between Minehead and Blue Anchor in March 1976. Operations were extended to Williton in August 1976, to Stogumber in May 1978, and to Bishops Lydeard in June 1979.

Steam and diesel trains run regularly over the 20 miles between Minehead and Bishops Lydeard, while the stretch of track between Bishops Lydeard and Norton Fitzwarren – connecting with the BR main line – is used for occasional special trains. The West Somerset Railway is Britain's longest preserved line.

The WSR runs through some of the finest scenery in the west country, ranging from the coastal plain and beaches of Blue Anchor Bay to the Quantock Hills. It is as varied, interesting and beautiful as that to be found on any railway in England. The stations all possess their own particular charm and are quite different in character, a fact that enhances the WSR's proud claim to be a railway with a unique branch line atmosphere, which not only provides a tourist attraction to visitors, but also serves the local community. The railway also has a very interesting collection of locomotives and rolling stock.

This book is a tribute to all those people whose enthusiasm and dedication over the years has ensured that the West Somerset Railway is now one of Britain's most popular and successful private lines. It is essentially in three parts. The first takes a glimpse at the Minehead branch in BR days, followed by a selection of photographs depicting the line in the early preservation years. The third part takes the reader on a journey along the line from Minehead to Norton Fitzwarren in more recent times.

The portfolio of photographs has been chosen from many submitted to portray the beauty of the scenery along the line, and feature a wide and balanced variety of locations and trains. Sincere thanks are due to all those photographers whose work adorns these pages. I am also grateful to John Pearce, whose commitment and enthusiasm got the whole project off the ground in the first place. Finally, if reading this book gives you as much pleasure and satisfaction as I have had in compiling it then all the hard work will have been well worthwhile.

April 1992

Richard Jones
Milverton, Somerset

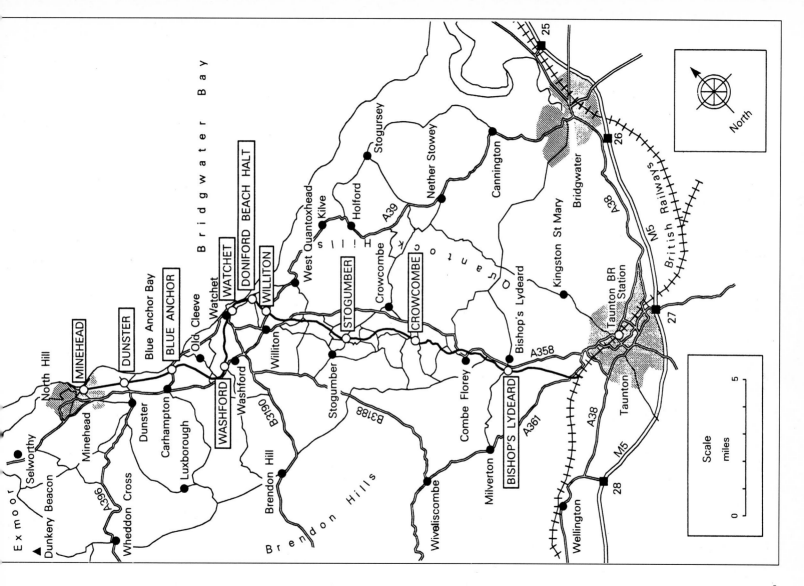

North

Bridgwater Bay

Exmoor

MINEHEAD
DUNSTER
BLUE ANCHOR
WASHFORD
WATCHET
DONIFORD BEACH HALT
WILLITON
STOGUMBER
CROWCOMBE
BISHOP'S LYDEARD

Scale
miles

0   5

3

BRITISH RAIL ERA

Taunton station

Left: The Bristol & Exeter Railway reached Taunton in July 1842. By 1873 the station had grown to become the junction station for four branch lines — those to Minehead, Barnstaple, Yeovil and Chard — in addition to serving trains on the B&ER main line. In steam days the station was a hive of activity. On 11 August 1962 ex-GWR 2-6-0 No 7326 awaits departure from one of the down bay platforms with a Barnstaple train, as another 'Mogul', No 7337, arrives from Barnstaple. *Peter W. Gray*

Norton Fitzwarren

Right: Norton Fitzwarren some 2¼ miles to the west of Taunton station, was the junction for both the Minehead and Barnstaple branches. In 1931, after track quadrupling from Taunton, the station was rebuilt with two island platforms. These were linked by footbridge to the station buildings on the up side. The station closed in 1964. Rationalisation of the track layout was in progress on 3 February 1965, as North British Type 2 diesel-hydraulic No D6320 comes off the Minehead branch and passes the Railway Hotel with an inspection saloon in tow. *Rev Hillary Dunn*

Bishops Lydeard

Left: BR Standard 2-6-2T No 82030 runs into the up platform at Bishops Lydeard with the 2.20pm Minehead-London Paddington train on 20 September 1963, as a three-car DMU approaches from Taunton. Taunton shed received a small fleet of these tank engines in the early 1960s for branch line work. The station was opened in March 1862 when the original West Somerset Railway was opened through to Watchet. The track between Bishops Lydeard and the junction at Norton Fitzwarren was doubled by the GWR in 1936.
Peter W. Gray

Crowcombe

Right: Crowcombe, just over seven miles from Norton Fitzwarren, is beautifully situated on the western slopes of the Quantock Hills and, at 400ft above sea level, is the highest point on the line. On 24 August 1963 GWR '5101' class 2-6-2T No 4143 has just passed through the station and is accelerating down the 1 in 81 gradient towards Taunton with the 2.20pm Minehead-Paddington train. This helps to explain why the engine is displaying 'A' class express-train lamps. These 'Large Prairie' tanks were regularly seen on the branch in GWR and BR days. *Peter W. Gray*

Leigh Bridge Loop

Left: The Great Western made a number of improvements to the Minehead branch during the 1930s. These included the installation of two additional passing loops — at Kentsford, between Watchet and Washford, and at Leigh Bridge, near Stogumber. The signalbox at Leigh Bridge was switched-out most of the time, but was opened to provide extra capacity at peak times in the summer. On 24 August 1963 GWR 2-6-2T No 4143 coasts downhill past the loop at the head of the 8.15am through train from London Paddington to Minehead (*above left*). Later the same day, and with the signalbox now switched-in, a three-car DMU on the 3.25pm Taunton-Minehead service passes a 'Hymek' Type 3 diesel-hydraulic, No D7046, waiting in the loop with the 3.10pm Minehead-Paddington train (*below left*). DMUs had replaced steam on local trains by 1963, while the 'Hymeks' were regularly used on through passenger and freight trains. *Peter W. Gray*

Stogumber

Right: Stogumber station was located deep in the heart of the West Somerset countryside and was over a mile from the the village it was built to serve. Opened in March 1862, the station was unusual in that the main station building was located on the opposite side of the track to the single platform. 'Hymek' No D7007 departs from the station and heads up the gradient towards Crowcombe at the head of the 11.15am service from Minehead to Paddington on 24 August 1963. Stogumber had its own camping coach for many years; this is visible in the background in front of the goods shed. *Peter W. Gray*

Williton

Left: The station at Williton, 15 miles from Taunton, was the principal crossing place on the Minehead branch. The station staff find time to talk to the passengers and engine crew as GWR '57xx' 0-6-0PT No 8745 waits on the up platform with the 10.50am Minehead-Taunton train on 31 May 1961. These pannier tanks were a regular sight on the branch. *Gerald T. Robinson*

Near Watchet

Above: GWR '61xx' 2-6-2T No 6113 rounds the curve at Doniford on the outskirts of Watchet with a Swansea-Minehead train (1.50pm ex-Taunton) on 24 August 1963. A handful of these 'Large Prairie' tanks were sent to Taunton shed in the later 1950s, having been displaced from London area suburban services, for which they were built, by DMUs. *Peter W. Gray*

DMU leaving Dunster

Above: A three-car cross country diesel multiple-unit departs from
Dunster, last stop before the branch terminus at Minehead, with an
afternoon local train from Taunton on 7 September 1968. The train is seen
taking the former up road on the double track section between Dunster
and Minehead, a consequence of track and signalling alterations brought
into use in September 1966, when the double line was converted to two
independent single lines running to the main and bay platforms at
Minehead, controlled by Dunster signalbox. *Peter W. Gray*

Minehead

Right: 'Hymek' Type 3 diesel-hydraulic No D7042 awaits departure from
Minehead with the daily Class 9 goods train to Taunton on 6 February
1964. The roof of the goods shed can be seen in the background above the
train, while the station yard, complete with crane, looks rather empty on
the right. Goods traffic on the branch was withdrawn by British Railways
just five months later. *Rev Hillary Dunn*

Reopening year

Left and right: The West Somerset Railway was opened amidst great celebration at Easter 1976. The opening ceremony was performed by Lord Montagu of Beaulieu. Train services initially ran the 3 ½ miles between Minehead and Blue Anchor, but were extended through to Williton in August of that year. Bagnall 0-6-0ST No 2996 *Victor* departs from Dunster in fine style on 25 August 1976 with an up train (*left*), while three months earlier the same locomotive leaves Dunster and takes the former up road with a Blue Anchor-Minehead train (*right*). *Victor*, restored at first in lined maroon livery, was a regular performer on WSR trains over many years, while the coaching stock was initially repainted in the company's colours of red and cream. Dunster signalbox was moved by rail to Minehead in 1977, where it is now in full operational use. *Rev Hillary Dunn (left) and Peter W. Gray (right)*

Minehead station

Left: A general view of the branch terminus at Minehead from the buffer stops not long after reopening, with a variety of rolling stock on display. On the left is GWR '64xx' 0-6-0PT No 6412, which was purchased from the Dart Valley Railway in early 1976 and saw regular service during the first three seasons of the WSR. It was withdrawn for overhaul in 1978. In the former goods shed, which was converted to serve as the railway's workshop, is GWR 2-6-2T No 4561 undergoing restoration, while 'Hymek' Type 3 diesel-hydraulic No D7017 and a Park Royal two-car DMU can be seen beyond the platform in the right background.*Peter W. Gray*

Awaiting restoration

Above: With a view to enhancing the steam locomotive fleet, the West Somerset Railway Association — the railway's principal support organisation — purchased a trio of ex-GWR 'Small Prairie' tank engines from Woodham's scrapyard at Barry in early 1976 for future use on the line. Two of the engines, '4575' 2-6-2Ts Nos 5521 and 5542, await loving attention at Bishops Lydeard soon after arrival in May 1976. The third member of the trio, No 4561 (one of the original '45xx' class) was restored to service in 1989 and has been a regular performer on WSR trains since then. Train services were not extended through to Bishops Lydeard until June 1979. *Peter W. Gray*

Kentsford

Left: Bagnall 0-6-0ST No 2994 *Vulcan* steams through the trees and past the farm crossing at Kentsford, between Watchet and Washford, with the 3.15pm Williton-Minehead train on 20 May 1978. The GWR installed an additional passing loop here in 1933, but this was taken out of use by British Railways in 1964 and the trackwork lifted. Both *Vulcan* and *Victor* were two of a trio of industrial saddle tanks originally built by W. G. Bagnall Ltd in 1951 for use at Margam Steelworks, Port Talbot, and purchased by the WSR from the former Austin Motor Co at Longbridge, near Birmingham. *Stephen Edge*

Winter landscape

Right: With all the main roads in the area closed because of the severe weather, one of the railway's two-car Park Royal DMUs crosses Sea Lane crossing at Dunster on 23 January 1979 with a relief train. Two of these DMUs were purchased from BR in the mid-1970s to help fulfil the WSR's original intention of running a regular local service over the line. Sea Lane once had traditional wooden gates operated by a crossing-keeper, who lived in the adjacent cottage. *Stephen Edge*

Bagnall power

Above: Bagnall 0-6-0ST No 2994 *Vulcan*, in unlined black livery, forges
past Castle Hill, between Williton and Stogumber, in September 1980 at
the head of a passenger train from Minehead to Bishops Lydeard.
Although both industrial saddle tanks saw regular service on the WSR
over many years, this view highlights how the locomotives — with their
short wheelbase and large cylinders — were not very well suited for
operation over a 20-mile line with steep gradients. *Peter W. Gray*

Industrial sunset

Right: A striking portrait of the industrial saddle tank *Victor* bathed in
early evening sunlight as it approaches the crossing at Leigh Wood at the
head of the 'Quantock Pullman' dining train in November 1980. This train
was the forerunner of the highly successful 'Quantock Belle', which has
done much to spearhead the railway's advance in recent years.
John Pearce

Two of a kind

Left: Both of the two Bagnall 0-6-0STs — No 2996 *Victor* leading No 2994 *Vulcan* — have steam to spare as they blow off furiously awaiting departure from Bishops Lydeard with a train for Minehead in August 1982. Double-heading with the two industrials was comparatively rare on the WSR. With the introduction of several ex-BR classes more suited to the line from the mid-1980s, the two Bagnalls were sold and moved on to pastures new — *Vulcan* in 1986 and *Victor* two years later — after many years of faithful service. *Stuart Trott*

Blue Anchor departure

Above: Former British Rail Class 14 diesel-hydraulic No 9551 leaves the picturesque station at Blue Anchor and commences the climb of Washford bank with the 10.15am Minehead-Bishops Lydeard service during the spring of 1984. The two-tone green livery of the locomotive and the chocolate-and-cream coaches reflect a deliberate change in policy at that time to portray the WSR as a more typical West Country branch line. *Richard Jones*

Through the trees

Left: Bagnall 0–6–0ST No 2994 *Vulcan* ventures through the undergrowth at Leigh Woods, on the climb between Stogumber and Crowcombe, with a Minehead to Bishops Lydeard service in April 1984, its last season in use on the line. The locomotive was later sold and departed from the railway in 1986. *Malcolm Short*

The local passenger

Right: The Great Western branch line recreated ... GWR '64xx' 0-6-0PT No 6412 steams past Doniford on the approach to Williton on 10 November 1984 on its way from Minehead to Bishops Lydeard to haul a special train to commemorate the locomotive's 50th anniversary. The engine had just returned to service following completion of a heavy overhaul. No 6412's return to service represented the start of a marked change in fortunes for the West Somerset Railway. *Richard Jones*

LATER PRESERVATION ERA

The start of the day

Below: Early morning at Minehead shed on 13 April 1991. A busy day is in prospect as five steam engines are prepared for the day's work ahead — GWR 0-6-0 No 3205, GWR '64xx' 0-6-0PT No 6412, GWR '45xx' 2-6-2T No 4561, GWR '61xx' 2-6-2T No 6106 and S&DJR '7F' 2-8-0 No 53808.
Richard Jones

Minehead shed

Right: A sunny day is in prospect as the ex-Somerset & Dorset '7F' No 53808 and two ex-GWR tanks, 0-6-0PT No 6412 and 2-6-2T No 4561, are prepared for service in September 1990. Minehead is the WSR's main steam locomotive maintenance and repair depot. The former goods shed — seen in the background — serves as the railway's workshop.
Alan Turner

Raising steam

Right: A view of the footplate of GWR 0-6-0 No 3205, the only surviving locomotive of its type, with the fireman in the process of making up the fire at the start of the day. Steam crews normally book on duty some three to four hours before departure of the first train. *Stephen Edge*

Minehead station

Above: A colourful scene at Minehead on 24 March 1991, with GWR '45xx' 2-6-2T No 4561 on station pilot duties. North Hill dominates the background. Opened in 1874, Minehead station boasts one long island platform, with the station buildings at the terminal end adjacent to the sea front. *David Mark ARPS*

No 53808 leaving Minehead

Right: The crew of S&DJR '7F' No 53808 receive instructions from the signalman at Minehead on 31 August 1991 as the 5.15pm departure commences its 20-mile journey to Bishops Lydeard. *Bryan Hicks*

Dunster

Above: GWR '64xx' 0-6-0PT No 6412 coasts into Dunster, first station out from Minehead, with an up train in May 1989. Nearby is Dunster Castle, home for centuries of the Luttrell family, promoters of the Minehead Railway, which explains the imposing entrance to a small country station. Dunster station is the home of the WSR's Ticket Printing Department.

Steam in the landscape

Right: Between Dunster and Blue Anchor the railway runs alongside Blue Anchor Bay and, on a clear day, the South Wales coast can be seen from passing WSR trains. GWR '64xx' 0-6-0PT No 6412 is dwarfed by the surrounding landscape at it approaches Blue Anchor station in October 1991. *Peter Doel*

Blue Anchor arrival

Left: The 10.15am departure from Minehead coasts into the up platform at Blue Anchor station on 6 May 1991, with the Somerset & Dorset '7F' 2-8-0 No 53808 at the helm. The station adjoins the beach and the signalbox controls the only wheel-operated gated crossing left in the West Country. *John Robinson*

The country station

Below and right: Two views of Blue Anchor station, which was opened on 16 July 1874 when the line was extended from the previous terminus at Watchet to Minehead. The splendid station gardens are seen to good effect (*below*) in June 1991, whilst the scene inside the signalbox (*right*) confirms that there is much more of interest on the West Somerset Railway than just the steam locomotives. Blue Anchor has received a Special Commendation in the national Best Restored Station Competition run by the Association of Railway Preservation Societies. *Richard Jones*

Trains crossing

Above: Evoking memories of the Minehead branch in Great Western times, '61xx' 2-6-2T No 6106 on the afternoon goods train to Williton passes '2251' class 0-6-0 No 3205 heading the 2.10pm Bishops Lydeard-Minehead train at Blue Anchor station on 5 September 1991. The waiting room on the down platform now houses the Blue Anchor Railway Museum, which is well worth a visit. *Jon Trott*

Washford bank

Right: From Blue Anchor the line curves inland and up Washford bank, much of it on a gradient of 1 in 65. A Cravens-built two-car DMU coasts down the bank and approaches Blue Anchor on 12 October 1991. In the background is the village of Old Cleeve. Whilst most trains on the West Somerset Railway are steam hauled, some off-peak services are regularly worked by DMUs. *Roger Penny*

Black Monkey bridge

Left: Bathed in sunshine GWR '64xx' 0-6-0PT No 6412 crosses Black Monkey bridge, which is situated about half way up Washford bank, in fine style on 27 September 1991 with the 2.05pm Minehead-Bishops Lydeard train. No 6412, owned by the West Somerset Railway Association, has been a regular performer on WSR services over many years. *Brian Dean*

Washford station

Below: GWR '61xx' 2-6-2T No 6106 coasts into Washford station on 25 August 1991 with a Minehead-bound train. Washford is the home of the Somerset & Dorset Railway Trust, owners of '7F' 2-8-0 No 53808. The shed and sidings in the background hold an interesting collection of rolling stock, including Peckett 0-4-0ST No 1788 *Kilmersdon*, while a museum of S&D artefacts has been established in the station building and former signalbox. *Stuart Trott*

Permanent way work

Right: With assistance from Stothert & Pitt steam-crane No 312, members of the Permanent Way Department install a new lead to the sidings at Washford on 24 February 1985. *Malcolm Short*

The branch line goods

Left: The branch line goods perfectly recreated. GWR '64xx' 0-6-0PT No 6412 approaches Washford with a Williton-Minehead goods train on 15 September 1985. Demonstration freight trains have been a regular feature of the railway's popular Gala Weeks in recent years.
Richard Jones

Watchet

Right: The West Somerset Railway is the home of many former Western Region diesel-hydraulic locomotives. One of these, 'Western' Type 4 No D1035 *Western Yeoman*, in desert sand livery, pulls away from the station at Watchet on 17 March 1991. The locomotive is actually No D1010 *Western Campaigner* but runs as No D1035 in recognition that it is owned by Foster Yeoman. The position of the station buildings provides a reminder that Watchet was the terminus of the original West Somerset Railway from Taunton before the extension to Minehead was opened.
Roger Penny

179

No 4561 passes Watchet docks

Left: Watchet is the oldest commercial port in the county of Somerset and was the main reason for building the original West Somerset Railway, which was opened in 1862. The town celebrated its millenium in 1988. On 7 September 1990 GWR '45xx' 2-6-2T No 4561 passes the harbour, where the *Gimo Dettica* is berthed, and approaches the station with the 10.20am Bishops Lydeard-Minehead train. Watchet is a popular destination for WSR passengers. *Bryan Hicks*

Doniford

Above: Passengers from Minehead get their last glimpse of the sea at Doniford, between Watchet and Williton, before the line curves inland towards Bishops Lydeard and Taunton. The popular GWR '64xx' 0-6-0PT No 6412 is seen at Doniford with the 2.05pm up train from Minehead on 10 August 1989. The WSR built a halt here, opened in 1988, to serve a nearby holiday camp. *Brian Dean*

Tank engines at Williton

Above left: Williton station is the principal crossing place on the West Somerset Railway. On 7 September 1991 GWR '61xx' 2-6-2T No 6106 waits in the down platform as GWR '45xx' 2-6-2T No 4561 approaches with a train from Minehead. Normally based at the Didcot Railway Centre, No 6106 spent the 1991 season operating on the WSR. *Roger Penny*

Colour

Below left: At the rear of the up platform at Williton station is the prize winning ancient maze garden of Highbridge House, a garden which is ablaze with colour throughout the summer. It is seen here on 25 August 1991. The station building, goods shed — which is now the home of the Diesel & Electric Preservation Group — and waiting room can be seen to the left. *Stuart Trott*

Awaiting departure

Right: S&DJR '7F' 2-8-0 No 53808 blows off impatiently as it awaits departure from Williton with the 4pm train from Minehead to Bishops Lydeard on 28 May 1989. The buildings on the down platform date from the opening of the line in March 1862 and are a perfect example of Bristol & Exeter Railway architecture. The signalbox is the only remaining operational B&ER example in the country. *Mark Wilkins*

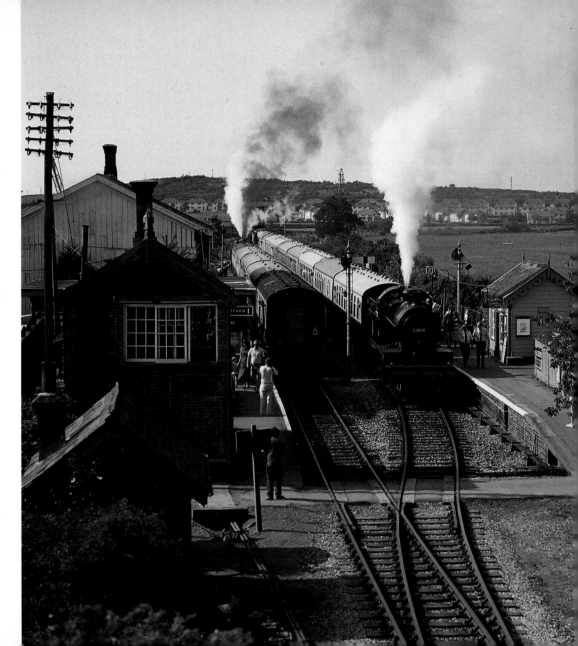

'Hymek' power

Left: 'Hymek' Type 3 diesel-hydraulic No D7017, beautifully restored in its original BR two-tone green livery, approaches Williton's down home signal with the 1.30pm Bishops Lydeard-Minehead train on 6 September 1987, the first day of the railway's 1987 Gala Week. No D7017 is one of two 'Hymeks' preserved by the Diesel & Electric Preservation Group; both are based on the WSR. *Peter W. Gray*

Evening Star

Right: The last steam locomotive built by British Railways, Class '9F' 2-10-0 No 92220 *Evening Star*, is now part of the National Collection and spent the 1989 season working passenger trains on the West Somerset Railway. The locomotive was turned out from Swindon Works in March 1960 and its appearance on the WSR proved both very popular and very successful. With its brunswick green paintwork gleaming No 92220 steams past Castle Hill with the 2.05pm Minehead-Bishops Lydeard service on 26 March 1989. *Brian Dean*

No 53808 near Woolston Moor

Above: Recalling days when the locomotive occasionally worked passenger trains over the steep gradients between Bath and Bournemouth, S&DJR '7F' 2-8-0 No 53808 storms uphill near Woolston Moor, between Williton and Stogumber, on 5 May 1991 at the head of the 4pm Minehead-Bishops Lydeard train. No 53808 has run in excess of 23,000 miles since its return to service from scrapyard condition in August 1987.

John Robinson

Evening sunshine

Right: The popular GWR '2251' class 0-6-0 No 3205 pauses at Bicknoller in the early evening of 22 June 1991 whilst hauling the 'Quantock Belle' dining train on its outward journey from Bishops Lydeard to Minehead. The Saturday evening 'QB' trains have a booked stop here to give diners outstanding views of the surrounding countryside whilst enjoying their meals. No 3205 is the only preserved example of a class of 120 0-6-0s built between 1930 and 1948. *Richard Jones*

No 6412 at Stogumber

Left: GWR '64xx' 0–6–0PT No 6412 makes a spirited departure from the highly picturesque station at Stogumber with the 2,05pm Minehead to Bishops Lydeard on the bright spring afternoon of 24 March 1991. No 6412 has been a regular and popular performer on the line since its reopening in 1976 and is owned by the West Somerset Railway Association. Stogumber, like all WSR stations, is staffed and maintained by volunteers. *Roger Penny*

Stogumber station

Right: Located deep in the heart of the West Somerset countryside, over a mile from the village it was built to serve, Stogumber is the only station on the WSR where the main station building is on the opposite side of the track to the platform. 'Hymek' diesel-hydraulic No D7017 approaches with a down train in March 1990. *Richard Jones*

Floral display

Right: The station gardens and floral displays are a feature of Stogumber through the summer and the subject of many favourable comments from visitors. On 24 August 1991 the main station building is awash with colour. The gardens and picnic area are on the site of the former station goods shed. *Richard Jones*

Through the trees

Left: With steam to spare, BR Class '9F' 2-10-0 No 92220 *Evening Star* steams uphill through Leigh Woods, near Stogumber, on 7 September 1989 at the head of the 10.15am Minehead-Bishops Lydeard train. The visit of *Evening Star* to the WSR for the 1989 season created a tremendous upsurge of interest in the line. *Bryan Hicks*

Leigh Woods

Right: A quartet of two-car DMUs approach Leigh Woods crossing with the 5.05pm Bishops Lydeard-Minehead service on 4 September 1988. Leigh Woods is one of two crossings between Stogumber and Crowcombe. These were previously gated and operated by crossing keepers who lived in tiny cottages alongside the line. This is the only occasion on which four DMUs have worked together on the West Somerset Railway. *Peter W. Gray*

Idyllic scenery

Above: '45xx' 2-6-2T No 4561 climbs through the countryside near Roebuck crossing with an empty coaching stock working to Bishops Lydeard on 2 September 1990 at the start of the railway's Gala Week. The West Somerset coast can be glimpsed in the background. *Peter Doel*

No 4561 approaches the summit

Right: The driver of GWR '45xx' 2-6-2T No 4561 shuts off steam as an up train approaches Crowcombe station, the highest point of the West Somerset Railway, on 9 September 1990. Two items of Great Western rolling stock add considerable character to the scene, while the former stationmaster's house can be seen immediately to the right of the locomotive. *Stuart Trott*

Crowcombe Heathfield station

Left: In its first full season of operation on the West Somerset Railway, GWR '2251' Class 0-6-0 No 3205 steams into the attractive station of Crowcombe with the 10.15am train from Minehead to Bishops Lydeard on 27 July 1988. As with Stogumber, the gardens are a feature of the station, whilst a small trackwork display established on the down platform can be seen in the background. The re-establishment of Crowcombe Heathfield as a regular passing place for WSR trains is likely in the near future. *Richard Jones*

Steam in the Quantocks

Right: Between Williton and Bishops Lydeard the West Somerset Railway runs alongside the Quantock Hills in contrast to the coastal scenery elsewhere on the line. In this delightful scene on 21 May 1991, GWR '61xx' 2–6–2T No 6106 momentarily disturbs the peace and tranquility at Nethercott as it climbs towards Crowcombe with the 3.45pm Bishops Lydeard to Minehead. *Brian Dean*

Santa special

Left: Bathed in glorious winter sunshine, GWR '4575' class 2–6–2T No5572 steams past Watersmeet, near Bishops Lydeard, on December 14 1986 while on its way to Crowcombe with a Santa special. Such trains are a regular and popular feature of the WSR calendar. No 5572, normally based at Didcot Railway Centre, worked on the West Somerset Railway in 1986 and 1987, evoking memories of the past as Taunton shed had a number of '4575' class engines on its books for branch line work. *Peter Doel*

No 92220 at Combe Florey

Above: On a glorious summer's day the visiting BR Standard Class '9F' 2-10-0 No 92220 *Evening Star* coasts downhill past Combe Florey and over the main Taunton-Minehead road with the 2.05pm departure from Minehead to Lydeard on 8 August 1989. Combe Florey was, for many years, the home of the writer Evelyn Waugh, perhaps now best-known as the writer of *Brideshead Revisited*, and the connection is maintained today by his son, Auberon, who continues to live there. *Brian Dean*

57

Bishops Lydeard

Left: Bishops Lydeard was once the last station on the branch from Minehead before the main line junction at Norton Fitzwarren, but since 1979 it has served as the southern terminus for passenger trains on the West Somerset Railway. The majority of the station buildings are on the down platform, as seen in this portrait of the station in April 1989 (*above left*). The station has also been the focus of many special events, most noticeably the annual Vintage Transport Rally organised by the West Somerset Railway Association. A superb line-up of traction engines can be seen on display at the 1991 Rally (*below left*). *Richard Jones*

Crowds

Double-headed departure

Left: The Great Western combination of '61xx' 2-6-2T No 6106 and '2251' 0-6-0 No 3205 make a spirited departure from the southern end of Bishops Lydeard on 13 April 1991 at the head of a British Rail through train which had originated at Hull. The operation of such through trains has done much to open up the West Somerset Railway to a wide audience. *Stuart Trott*

Works train

Right: The West Somerset Railway has nearly 23 miles of running line to maintain and keep in good condition. Engineers' works trains are regularly seen on the line, particularly through the winter months, to assist with the task. Sentinel 0-6-0 diesel No 57 is seen at Dene Bridge, south of Bishops Lydeard, on 9 March 1989 on such a duty. *Peter W. Gray*

Pullman special

Above: With a rake of 13 coaches in tow, including some Pullman stock, S&DJR '7F' 2-8-0 No 53808 and GWR '2251' 0-6-0 No 3205 coast past Longlands Farm bridge on the return leg of a through train to Paddington on 24 March 1991. This was the first such train to run between London and Minehead for 21 years. Clear evidence of the double track between Norton Fitzwarren and Bishops Lydeard can be seen at this point.

62   *Richard Jones*

Steam meets diesel

Right: 16 June 1990 was a very significant day for the West Somerset Railway. GWR '64xx' 0-6-0PT No 6412 and '45xx' 2-6-2T No 4561 stand at the end of the Minehead branch at Norton Fitzwarren, awaiting the arrival of a special train from Manchester — this was the first train to work through from British Rail on to WSR metals. An InterCity 125 express passes by on an up train and the scene makes a very interesting comparison with that on page 5. *Richard Jones*

Tailpiece

Sunset over Blue Anchor; 7 May 1989. *Stuart Trott*